How to Hear the Voice of God
Voice of God

Workbook

COLETTE TOACH

AMI BOOKSHOP

www.ami-bookshop.com

How to Hear the Voice of God Workbook

ISBN-10: 1626640858
ISBN-13: 978-1-62664-085-6

1st Printing September 2014

Published by **AMI Bookshop**
E-mail Address: admin@ami-bookshop.com
Web Address: www.ami-bookshop.com

Scripture quotations are taken from the Apostolic Movement International (AMIV) version of the Bible.

How to Hear the Voice of God Workbook

Practical and to the point, this book has a single purpose – to draw you into a face-to-face relationship with the Lord Jesus. As you learn to hear the Lord's voice, you will come to experience Him.

Only then will you truly know of His love for you. It is one thing to read of the Lord's love but another to experience it. The more you hear His voice, the more you will come to know Him.

You will come to discover the Lord's character in a way you never have before. In fact, you will see that He has a personality and desires of His own.

There is so much that the Lord wants to tell you. He is pent up with secrets and sweet words on the tip of His tongue. All He is waiting for is for you to listen.

So come then, let me take you into the secret place. Come with all joy, because standing on the other side of this door is a Father that is proud of you, a Savior that adores you and a Spirit that is ready to bless you.

There is so much about the Lord that you do not know. You have known partially, but now you will know completely! Do not be surprised then as you walk across the threshold and come face-to-face with... yourself!

During the course of the following weeks you will see aspects to your own character that you did not know existed. In many ways, knowing how to hear the Lord's voice is intricately entwined in how well we know ourselves.

So allow the Lord Jesus to slowly remove the veils that have hidden His face from you. Allow the Holy Spirit to take away the noise that has hindered the direction He has for you. Only then will you enter into a realm you knew was there but were afraid you would never reach.

Keep this one thing in mind – as much as you want to hear the Lord's voice, He wants to fellowship with you. He stands right now at the door of your heart and knocks. Once you hear it, you can open that door and allow Him in.

So project by project, I am going to teach you the language of the Spirit. I am going to open your eyes to truths you might not have seen before.

Together we will enter into the secret place because it is in this place where you will hear the voice of God.

How to Use This Book

I have broken each project into clearly laid out headings. Although more appropriate for the local church or small group settings, you can also do these projects in your private time.

If you are not currently attending a church and you face a problem with these lessons, you are welcome to contact us. One of our ministers can help you out or refer you to a pastor in your area. (Apostolic Movement International – www.apostolic-movement.com)

Let me give you a brief description of what each of these headings mean so that you can move on quickly to your first project!

Corresponding Chapter
Keep in mind that this workbook is based on the *How to Hear the Voice of God* book. Each chapter will reference the corresponding chapter in that book. In addition to that, a few projects will also reference other materials available through our ministry.

Project Objective
This is a general outline of what the project is about.

Project Profile
Here you will find a bulleted list of who this project is appropriate for.

Project Outline
By far the lengthiest section of each project; here, I outline a full description of what the project is about, what you need to do and the results you should expect.

Project Submission
These questions will bring everything together. If you are doing this workbook in a group setting, these are the questions you will submit or bring along to your next meeting.

Outcome Assessment
A few words concluding the project; I also include the occasional note to the leader of the group study.

A Note to the Course Leaders

Because this book is designed as a church group study, I have tried to keep it as practical as possible. If you as a leader struggle with any of your group, you are welcome to contact us (Apostolic Movement International – www.apostolic-movement.com) for assistance.

Although most of the questions are self-explanatory we do understand that sometimes you might encounter situations you do not have the answer to. We will be able to refer you to either a resource or answer your questions ourselves.

If you are hosting this as a course in your church, we do suggest that each attendee has their own kit including the book and workbook. This will make things a lot easier for you.

If this is your first time hosting such a group, I suggest you also get your hands on my book Mentorship 101 for guidelines on how to work with individuals you will be mentoring personally.

Hosting a Study Group

My personal suggestion for working through this course as a group would be as follows:

1. Begin the course by holding a viewing of the bonus DVD entitled, *"Knowing God's Will"* and then follow up by reading the first project Hearing God Through the Word.
2. Make sure that the group knows that they have to read the first chapter in the book and complete the project in time for the next class.
3. Although you could ask the members to write down and e-mail you their completed projects, it would be easier if you had them read their answers out at the next class. This will allow for interaction.
4. You can choose to read the next chapter together or to get each person to do the reading at home, bringing the completed project to the next class.

By having the group each read out their answers, you will encourage ministry and interaction in the group. This will allow you to see if anyone is having a hard time with the studies and also to identify those that might show potential to host the class for the next group.

By all means feel free to skip a project or to add to it. Each group is different and you need to allow the Holy Spirit to lead you so that you can meet everyone's needs.

This is also a good time to mention that it is likely that through the course of this study that some budding prophetic ministers might start showing up. If so, you are welcome to take advantage of some of our other materials.

We have also found that most groups really enjoy the *Dreams and Visions* section of this study. A good follow up group would be to do the *Way of Dreams and Visions* church course which includes a book and workbook.

Time to Get Going

Well it is time to get moving then! Hopefully you have already started reading the *How to Hear the Voice of God* book and watched the bonus DVD. If so, you are ready to get started. You are ready to experience the Lord in a way you never have before!

Contents

PROJECT 1

Hearing God Through the Word

Project 1 – Hearing God Through the Word

*Hebrews 4:12 For the **word** of God [is] living, and powerful, and sharper than any two-edged sword, piercing even to the dividing apart of soul and spirit, and of the joints and marrow, and [is] a discerner of the thoughts and intents of the heart.*

Corresponding Chapter

The following project lines up with **Chapter 1: Hearing God Through the Word** from the *How to Hear the Voice of God* book.

It also corresponds with the **Knowing God's Will DVD** taken from the *Called to the Ministry* series

Project Objective

We are told from the time that we are born again to "get into the Word of God." There is quite a difference though between "getting into the Word" and the "Word getting into you!"

This project will teach you how to make the Word real in your every-day-life. Not only will it help you remember what you read, but it will infuse you with the kind of power that will renew your mind.

Project Profile

- Ideal for believers of every spiritual maturity
- Home church leaders
- Small group gatherings
- For someone called to a teaching ministry
- Ideal pastor-teacher project

Project Outline

Perhaps you are already familiar with how to read the Word in this way. If so, then this will add even more power to your spiritual life!

When I was looking to the Lord for more authority in my walk, He directed me to His Word.

He showed me again and again that if I wanted to increase the measure of faith and authority I had, it meant getting the Word into me! It was through this process that I came to know Jesus through the Word. Here I discovered that the Word was a living and breathing thing!

It is not just words on a page. It holds the power to transform your mind, divide the soul and spirit and bring fire from heaven! Well, how do you think this kind of transformation is going to come to pass?

Without realizing it, there are already many things that have molded your character and abilities through the years. The things you have studied and meditated on have shaped the way you view life. If you always meditated on good things, you will have a positive outlook. The opposite holds true of course if you always had a negative view on life.

Well, imagine for a moment if the things you dwell on not only changed the way you view life but actually contained real power to change your circumstances? Well, that is the power that the Word of God holds! Not only does visualizing the Scriptures hold the power to transform your mind but as you allow this transformation to take place, it adds power to your spirit to change your very life.

What problems do you have right now? Do you have a problem seeing the truth of your masculinity? Do you have a problem imagining that you are loved? Do you struggle with fear or anger?

When you close your eyes, how do you see yourself? Do you see the weaknesses and the lack in your life? Well, right now what you need is an overhaul! Well, that is what this project is about. It is going to "weight lift" your spirit to cause it to build new pictures in your mind.

We will start with some general passages, but as you do these, it is easy to pick out scriptures that apply directly to your problem.

1. Visualize this scripture:
Visualize and see yourself in this passage:

1 Kings 19:11 And he said, Go out, and stand on the mountain before the LORD [Yahweh]. And the LORD [Yahweh] passed by, and a great and strong wind tore the mountains, and broke in pieces the rocks before the LORD [Yahweh]; [but] the LORD [Yahweh] [was] not in the wind: and after the wind an earthquake; [but] the LORD [Yahweh] [was] not in the earthquake:

12 And after the earthquake a fire; [but] the LORD [Yahweh] [was] not in the fire: and after the fire a still small voice.

13 And it was [so], when Elijah heard [it], that he wrapped his face in his mantle, and went out, and stood at the entrance of the cave. And, behold, [there came] a voice to him, and said, What are you doing here, Elijah? (AMIV)

1. What did you see?

_____

_____

_____

_____

_____

_____

_____

2.   What did you feel?

_____

_____

_____

_____

_____

3.   What did God tell YOU through this passage?

_____

_____

_____

_____

_____

_____

2. Take these scriptures and:
   a. Visualize them
   b. Memorize them.

Psalms 18:2 The LORD [Yahweh] [is] my rock, and my fortress, and my deliverer; my God, my strength, in whom I will trust; my buckler, and the horn of my salvation, [and] my high tower. (AMIV)

Romans 8:31 What will we then say to these things? If God [be] for us, who [can be] against us?

32 He that spared not his own Son, but delivered him up for us all, how will he not with him also freely give us all things? (AMIV)

Matthew 7:9 Who is there amongst you, whom if his son asks for bread, will give him a stone?

10 Or if he asks for a fish, will he give him a snake?

11 If you then, being evil, know how to give good gifts to your children, how much more will your Father who is in heaven give good things to those that ask him? (AMIV)

3. Pick Out Your Own Passages

Now that you are getting the hang of visualizing the Word, it is time to bring it home. What are you struggling with right now? Depending on your current problems, pick out some relevant scriptures to meditate on.

For example if you always struggle seeing yourself as successful, a good passage to visualize would be:

Ecclesiastes 5:19 Every man also to whom God has given riches and wealth, and has given him power to eat of it, and to take his portion, and to rejoice in his labour; this [is] the gift of God.

If you struggle with self-image an awesome passage is:

Genesis 1:26 And God said, Let us make man in our image, after our likeness: and let them have dominion over the fish of the sea, and over the fowl of the air, and over the cattle, and over all the earth, and over every creeping thing that creeps upon the earth.

As you read that passage, you see yourself having the image of God and no longer see the failures in yourself!

Struggling with your health? There are many fantastic passages to dwell on, but here is an example:

Jeremiah 30:17 For I will restore health to you, and I will heal you of your wounds, says the LORD [Yahweh]; because they called you an Outcast, [saying], This [is] Zion, whom no man seeks after.

Now it's your turn. Pick out some passage relevant to your personal struggles today and begin visualizing and memorizing them!

Project Submission

Submit the following response to your leader:

1. Paint a picture of what you visualized with each passage.

_____

_____

_____

_____

_____

2. Did you find it easy to visualize the Word? If not, explain any blockages you had.

_____

_____

_____

_____

_____

3. Take this a step further and pick out 3 more passages to visualize and memorize that are applicable to your circumstances right now.

_____

_____

_____

_____

_____

Outcome Assessment

The first result in doing this project should be an immediate increase in faith. The more you meditate on these passages the more the positive pictures will replace the negative.

Each time that you feel tempted to think on the negative things, bring the new pictures to your mind that you used to build your faith. Bit by bit you will transform your mind!

Notes:

_____

_____

_____

_____

_____

Urim & Thummim

Project 2 – Urim and Thummim

Leviticus 8:8 And he put the breastplate upon him: also he put in the breastplate the Urim and the Thummim.

Corresponding Chapter

The following project lines up with **Chapter 2: Hearing God Through Urim and Thummim** from the *How to Hear the Voice of God* book.

Project Objective

You have been hearing the Lord's voice more than you realize! In fact, since you got born again, He has been speaking to you. All you need to do now is apply this to every area of your life. Use this project to identify when the Lord has been speaking to you using the Urim and Thummim.

Work through each table diligently and then submit the final report to your leader in the Project Submission section.

Project Profile

- New Converts
- Prophetic ministry
- Intercessory group
- Someone needing direction
- Great for home church and small group gatherings

Project Outline

This project is quite simple. What you will do for the following week is to determine when the Lord is giving you direction using your Urim and Thummim. Remember to refer back to the book for the teaching on this, alright?

For now, let's see where the Lord has been giving you a "yes" or "no" in various areas of your life. Do not be concerned if you do not get anything. During these times there are two possible reasons.

When God does not give anything, either the timing is wrong or He is saying, "You choose!" For now though, let's determine how the Lord has been leading you so far in the following 3 areas of your life:

1. Prayer Life
As you come to prayer this week, fill in this table explaining what you brought to the Lord and whether you felt a Urim or Thummim on whether you should pray it through or not.

Please use table the on next page.

Weekday	Prayer Request	Urim or Thummim
Monday	_____ _____ _____ _____ _____ _____ _____	
Tuesday	_____ _____ _____ _____ _____ _____ _____	
Wednesday	_____ _____ _____ _____ _____ _____ _____	

Thursday		
	_____	
	_____	
	_____	
	_____	
	_____	
Friday		
	_____	
	_____	
	_____	
	_____	
	_____	
Saturday		
	_____	
	_____	
	_____	
	_____	
	_____	
Sunday		
	_____	
	_____	
	_____	
	_____	
	_____	
	_____	

2. Workplace

We make decisions all the time. Use this project to list at least one decision you had to make every day this week and what you felt in your spirit. If you stay at home, you can also include decisions around that.

Please use table the on next page.

Weekday	Prayer Request	Urim or Thummim
Monday	_____ _____ _____ _____ _____	
Tuesday	_____ _____ _____ _____ _____	
Wednesday	_____ _____ _____ _____ _____	
Thursday	_____ _____ _____ _____ _____	

Friday		
	_____	
	_____	
	_____	
	_____	
	_____	
	_____	
Saturday		
	_____	
	_____	
	_____	
	_____	
	_____	
	_____	
Sunday		
	_____	
	_____	
	_____	
	_____	
	_____	
	_____	

3. Your Daily Life

Now bring the Lord into your family and natural life. What decisions did you have to make regarding your circumstances, children or direction for life? List one or more decisions you had to make each day and what you felt in your spirit.

Weekday	Prayer Request	Urim or Thummim
Monday	_____ _____ _____ _____ _____	
Tuesday	_____ _____ _____ _____ _____	
Wednesday	_____ _____ _____ _____ _____	
Thursday	_____ _____ _____ _____ _____	

Friday		
	_____	
	_____	
	_____	
	_____	
	_____	
	_____	
	_____	
Saturday		
	_____	
	_____	
	_____	
	_____	
	_____	
	_____	
	_____	
Sunday		
	_____	
	_____	
	_____	
	_____	
	_____	
	_____	
	_____	

Project Submission

After completing the project, submit the following answers to your leader during the next gathering.

1. Did you see a pattern in the decisions where the Lord gave you an Urim? Explain.

_____

_____

_____

_____

_____

2. Did you see a pattern in the decisions where the Lord gave you a Thummim? Explain.

_____

_____

_____

_____

_____

3. What are your conclusions on this project as a whole?

_____

_____

_____

_____

_____

_____

Outcome Assessment

Once you are able to sense when the Lord is saying "yes" or "no", you are well on your way to hearing Him in many other ways. So, take your time with this project until it becomes second nature. It will give you the assurance you need in your daily walk with the Lord.

Notes:

_____

_____

_____

_____

_____

Dream Interpretation

Project 3 – Dream Interpretation

Job 33:15 In a dream, in a vision of the night, when deep sleep falls upon men, in slumberings upon the bed;

Corresponding Chapter

The following project lines up with **Chapter 3: Hearing God Through Dreams** from the *How to Hear the Voice of God* book.

It also corresponds with the **Dream Interpretation by the Spirit DVD** taken from the *Way of Dreams and Visions* series.

Project Objective

The Lord uses dreams to speak to His people. This project will help you to sort through your dreams and help you to identify what is of Him and what is not. Before long, you will be uncovering the secret messages in your dreams!

Project Profile

- For every believer regardless of maturity
- Anyone in prophetic ministry
- Essential for all leaders
- Ideal for church study groups

Project Outline

A full explanation was provided in the *How to Hear the Voice of God* book, so we will bring all these points together so that you can outline your dream. It might seem labor intensive at the beginning, but as you get used to it, you will start to see how easy it is!

If you want to get more out of this, then I suggest you get your hands on *The Way of Dreams and Visions* book and workbook.

Let's Begin!

Begin this project by outlining a dream that you had recently that you remember. It is best to pick out a dream that was short and to the point. If the dream had too many scene changes, it is likely to be a purging dream and is also harder to work through.

Make things easy for yourself by starting with a dream that is simple and has just a few symbols that stood out to you.

Outline Your Dream Here:

Step 1: Categorizing Your Dreams

What category do you feel your dream falls into and why do you say that?

        a. External Prophetic
        b. Internal Prophetic
        c. Healing
        d. Garbage

My Dream Category is:

_____

_____

_____

_____

_____

_____

_____

Step 2: Identify the Spirit

What did you feel in the dream? Do you feel that the message is positive or negative? Give a brief description of how you felt in the dream.

The Spirit on My Dream Was:

_____

_____

_____

_____

_____

_____

_____

_____

_____

Step 3: Identifying the Symbols

Use the table below to list all the symbols in your dream and what they mean to you. Remember, for internal dreams, the symbols will reflect a part of yourself. For external dreams, the symbol meaning will be found in the Word.

Please use table the on next page.

	Places	Scenes	People	Objects	Creatures / Animals	Colors, Senses, Numbers
Describe Symbol						
What this symbol means to you in real life.						
For external – what the symbol means In the Word.						

Step 4: Your Final Revelation

Now that you have all these elements together, what do you believe your final interpretation is of this dream?

Project Submission

1.　　　Document your original dream.

_____

_____

_____

_____

_____

_____

2.　　　Document your final interpretation.

_____

_____

_____

_____

_____

_____

3.   Consider the emotion you felt in your dream. Is there an area of your life where you can identify this same feeling?

_____

_____

_____

_____

_____

4.   If you are submitting this project in a group setting, open it up for others in the group to include their own interpretations for your dream.

Outcome Assessment

This is a fantastic team building project, and I encourage you to do it in a group setting. It is difficult sometimes to get an interpretation for your own dream because of your mindsets. It is easier for someone looking in from the outside.

Because of this, it is a great idea to allow others to give you input. While not everyone will be correct, you will start to get the general idea of what the Lord is saying. On the flipside, you will also find it easier to interpret for others.

So if you found it a bit of a challenge to interpret for yourself, do not get discouraged. It takes time to understand the parables of the spirit! Do not give up though because the Lord will continue to speak to you in this way, and before long, you will get to the place where you wake up with the interpretation already mulling around in your head.

Notes:

_____

_____

_____

_____

_____

_____

_____

_____

_____

_____

_____

_____

_____

PROJECT 4

Hearing God Through Visions

Project 4 – Hearing God Through Visions

Acts 16:9 And a vision appeared to Paul in the night; There stood a man of Macedonia, and prayed him, saying, Come over into Macedonia, and help us.

Corresponding Chapter

The following project lines up with **Chapter 4: Hearing God Through Visions** from the *How to Hear the Voice of God* book.

It also corresponds with the **Experiencing the Realm of the Spirit Audio DVD** taken from the *Way of Dreams and Visions* series.

Project Objective

If you are spirit filled, it is quite likely that you have already experienced visions. Most people though expect something different to what they are. They are waiting for a trance vision without realizing that the impressions they are getting are in fact visions.

Remember the visualization project at the beginning of this book? By doing this, you are already learning the language of the Spirit! You are building pictures into your spirit that the Holy Spirit will use to get your attention.

So do not be surprised if you find some of those pictures popping up as you pray or minister. If they do... you are experiencing visions! The Lord is speaking in a language that you will understand.

Project Profile

- Every believer
- Prophetic minister
- Anyone wanting to flow in the gifts of the Spirit
- For someone used to flowing as a teacher and wanting to flow more in the realm of visions
- Prayer groups

- Perfect for any small group setting

Project Outline

The Lord will give you visions when you put yourself in a position to receive them. In other words, you will receive visions in prayer, ministry or even in praise and worship. Using these three categories, I want to help you start identifying the pictures that are in your mind.

Once you can identify that, you will be able to sort out which pictures are from the Lord and which ones are just something you imagined.

During Praise and Worship

When you come to the Lord in praise and worship, be mindful of the pictures you see. Sure, some of them might very well be images you made up – your imagination. However, you will soon discover pictures that you did not imagine yourself!

Please use table the on next page.

Describe the picture you visualized during praise and worship.	What impression did you get from this picture?	Does this picture line up with the Word?	Conclusion: Was this of the Lord?

During Prayer Times

Describe the picture you visualized during praise and worship.	What impression did you get from this picture?	Does this picture line up with the Word?	Conclusion: Was this of the Lord?

During Ministry

This project is optional because it is applicable for ministry leaders. If you are in a place to minister to someone else, then by all means do it. However, if you are not in a place to minister, you can skip it.

Please use table the on next page.

Describe the picture you visualized during praise and worship.	What impression did you get from this picture?	Does this picture line up with the Word?	Conclusion: Was this of the Lord?

Project Submission

Going through the three tables, submit the following results as your report.

1.   What visions did you receive that you feel were definitely of the Lord?

_____

_____

_____

_____

_____

2.   Include what you were praying for or doing at the time of receiving the vision.

_____

_____

_____

_____

_____

3.   Did the vision feel positive or negative?

_____

_____

_____

_____

_____

_____

4.   Looking at the symbols in those visions, what would you
say their interpretation is?

_____

_____

_____

_____

_____

_____

Outcome Assessment

Sometimes it takes a while to get the full interpretation of a vision.
The reason for this is often the timing of it. The Lord will unveil its

meaning over time. For the most part though, the more you know of the Word, the easier the interpretation will be.

Even if your vision is something you are familiar with, it will have its meaning deeply seated in the Scriptures. Refer to the *Way of Dreams and Visions Symbol Dictionary* to help you out with symbols you struggled with.

This project is fantastic to use in a group prayer meeting. Allow each one the opportunity to share what they see, and have the others judge whether they think it is of the Lord or not. This will make you accountable and also help you to know what is of the Lord and what is not.

Notes:

_____

_____

_____

_____

_____

_____

_____

_____

_____

The Second Wind Project

Project 5 – The Second Wind Project

> *Hebrews 12:1 There since we also are surrounded with so great a cloud of witnesses, let us lay aside every weight, and the sin which so easily besets [us], and let us run with endurance the race that is set before us,*

Corresponding Chapter

The following project lines up with **Chapter 5: Hearing God Through Tongues** from the *How to Hear the Voice of God* book.

Project Objective

Consider this project a spiritual workout that will make you trim and fit in no time at all! This project is designed to stretch you and to also arm you with a powerful spiritual weapon – the gift of tongues!

Project Profile

- For every believer
- Especially vital to anyone with a prophetic ministry
- Intercessors group

Project Outline

My father-in-law was a marathon runner. Pushing their bodies to extremes, each one understood the concept of the "second wind." It usually happened near the end of the race when they were so weary that they did not think they could go on any more.

When a runner has spent all his energy and feels like his legs cannot take another step, he can do one of two things. He can give up or push through to second wind. When he pushes past the exhaustion and the pain, he will switch over and suddenly the weariness will give way to a new boost of energy.

From feeling like giving up, he will get a boost to run faster than ever, just one last time. If he times it just right, he can finish his race with his second wind!

The same principle can be found in your spiritual life. As you pray and read the Word, you are exercising your spirit. However, there needs to come a time when you push it to the limit - When you tap into a greater source of power than you ever have before.

It will mean to keep pushing your spirit until you break into a new realm. There is only one way to do it, and it sounds simpler than it is.

What the Second Wind Feels Like
When you pray long enough in tongues, you will feel a surge in your spirit. It might feel like butterflies in your stomach. The anointing will increase, and the gifts of revelation will flow.

From feeling weary, your mind will be sparked off, and you will start flowing in visions or receiving a clear impression in your spirit from the Lord. When this happens, you know it is time to pray, decree and release whatever God wants you to.

The Process:

This project is simple and easy to do.

1. Speak in tongues for at least an hour
Now this might sound simple, but you will soon find that you will get weary. You have put a lot of junk into your spirit, and it has been a long time since you poured out a lot. As a result you will find speaking in tongues like this hard at first.

In fact, the longer it takes, the more your spirit has been overloaded with the things of the world. The objective of this project is to keep speaking in tongues until you experience that second wind.

There is good news though! You will only need to do this once. Once you have broken through to that second wind, and the revelations have started to flow, the next time that you start to pray, you will feel the presence of the Lord right away!

Project Submission

Submit the answers to the following questions to your group leader:

1.   How many times did you attempt the project before you broke through to second wind?

_____

_____

_____

_____

_____

_____

2.   How long did it take you to reach "second wind" the first time?

_____

_____

_____

_____

_____

3. Describe what "second wind" felt like to you.

_____

_____

_____

_____

4. What revelations or experiences did you have in the spirit that stood out to you during this project?

_____

_____

_____

_____

Outcome Assessment

There are many different outcomes for this project. The first, of course, is a breakthrough in the realm of the spirit. Depending on how long it has been since you really invested into your spirit, will depend on how long it takes.

For most students, you will experience a breakthrough in the spirit and will also operate in visions and some of the other ways of hearing the Lord. There are some though that hit a wall. Then, there are also others that experience demonic manifestations.

The reason for this is that if there is something demonic in their lives that has been hidden for a while. As you bring your spirit to life, anything that is not of the Lord will most certainly get uncomfortable.

If you are uncomfortable with anything that happens during this project, please contact your pastor or team leader right away. It is not uncommon for some to experience a spirit of divination or a spiritual blockage. Again, you will need counsel on how to break free – so do not be afraid to get help if you find yourself struggling.

A Note to the Leader

Depending on how long it takes your student to get a breakthrough will let you know how much time they spend in the spirit and how much they fill it with junk. This project is also a good challenge for you!

Like I already mentioned, there are some that will experience a demonic manifestation. If this does happen, you don't have to be concerned, but, you will need to follow up with counseling and help them break free. I suggest you refer to *The Minister's Handbook* for practical points on how to deal with this.

Notes:

_____

_____

_____

_____

_____

Bulldozing

Project 6 – Bulldozing

Ephesians 6:17 And take the helmet of salvation, and the sword of the spirit, which is the [rhema]word of God:

Corresponding Chapter

The following project lines up with **Chapter 5: Hearing God Through Tongues** from the *How to Hear the Voice of God* book.

Project Objective:

There is only one way that faith increases and that is by hearing the rhema word of God. A powerful weapon for every believer, this project will increase faith and assist in an answer to prayer.

Got a problem that you are having a hard time overcoming? This project is called the "bulldozing project" because it grows your faith to such a level that it literally levels that problem!

This is the best "emergency go to" when you are faced with a dire problem you cannot handle. Watch the Lord move as you build your faith using both the Word and the Spirit.

Take note that this project is not a magic wand. Rather it is a tool used to increase your faith. Faith in turn yields the answer to prayer.

Project Profile:

- Ideal for prophets in training
- Should be mandatory for intercessors
- Ideal for believers believing God for something specific
- Spiritual maturity
- Immediate solution for a current problem
- Faith builder

Bulldozing P a g e | **61**

Project Outline

My son loves bulldozers. If there is one on a construction site, he makes us slow the car so that he can get a better look. It is some impressive equipment. It can face a pile of rubble or even a heap of sand and push it over with no effort at all.

That is the picture you want to keep in mind as you approach this project. What is your problem today? What are you struggling with? This project will give you the bulldozer you need to run right through these problems.

Never forget, the Lord is moved by faith. Without faith it is impossible to please Him. So do you want an answer to your prayer? Then you need to get your faith into gear! Until you "know that you know" God has heard you, you will always have doubt.

So get ready to kick the doubt out and build your faith up. It is time to build yourself a bulldozer!

The Process

1. Go to the Word and pick out around 5 of your favorite promises. If you have a particular need, then select scriptures that are an answer to your need.
2. Write down each scripture on a card or piece of paper.
3. Find a quiet place and do the following:
   a. Begin by reading the scriptures out loud one at a time.
   b. As you read the scripture, visualize the pictures in it. For example if you are quoting "... whoever says to this mountain be removed... " see that mountain being taken from your path as you quote the passage.
   c. Once you have quoted the scriptures for about 5 minutes, put them down and spend the next five minutes speaking in tongues.
   d. Alternate speaking in tongues and quoting the scriptures, quoting for 5 minutes and speaking in tongues for 5 minutes.

How to Hear the Voice of God Project Book

4.   As you continue doing this, you will start to feel a stirring inside your spirit. When this happens, now is the time to pray and speak the will of God into your life.

Points to Keep in Mind:

- It is important to keep your mind focused on what you are doing. Visualize the scriptures and keep those pictures in mind when you are speaking in tongues.
- Only pray in English when you feel the build up in your spirit.
- If you have not done this before, it might take some time before you get the initial breakthrough.

Project Submission

Once you are finished submit the following report to your leader:

1. A list of the scriptures you picked out.

_____

_____

_____

_____

_____

_____

_____

2. What did you struggle with the most?

_____

_____

_____

_____

_____

3. What have you been believing God for?

_____

_____

_____

_____

_____

4. How long did it take you to feel a buildup on the inside?

_____

_____

_____

_____

5. What are your final feelings and conclusions on this project? What did you get out of it?

_____

_____

_____

_____

Outcome Assessment

Most believers that go through this project get a big breakthrough in their spiritual and natural lives. This is a great project to make a habit in your daily life. You can quote the Word and speak in tongues on the way to work or whenever you have a moment to yourself.

It is a powerful faith builder that no believer should be without.

A Note to the Leader

If your student struggled and did not get a breakthrough, then they have a spiritual blockage.

Of course, if they do not speak in tongues, this project will be a challenge. If they are not spirit-filled, then they can simply quote the scriptures and then pray. It will take them a bit longer, but they will still build their faith this way and see results.

Notes:

_____

_____

Hearing God Through Journaling

Project 7 – Hearing God Through Journaling

1 Chronicles 28:19 All [this, said David], the LORD [Yahweh] made me understand in writing by [his] hand upon me, [even] all the works of this pattern.

Corresponding Chapter

The following project lines up with **Chapter 6: Hearing God Through Journaling** from the *How to Hear the Voice of God* book.

Project Objective

Every believer should know how to journal. It is the first step towards a face-to-face relationship with Jesus. It is also essential when seeking the Lord for clear direction regarding a matter.

Having these moments with the Lord written down means you are able to come back later and test those words – seeing what was the Lord and what was not.

Project Profile

- For new believers
- For any believer who is trying to develop a face to face relationship with Jesus
- Decision making
- Learning to flow from the spirit

Project Outline

It helps to have an example to go on when journaling. I already teach you how to journal in the book so I will not expand on it here. Instead I will include an example of what a journal looks like so that you have a track to run on.

Journal Example:

Lord there has been so much warfare and also spiritual attacks. There is just so much to do here that I do not know where to begin. There is so much to organize that I feel overwhelmed. Lord please give me direction and wisdom.

I am the source of all living water, my child, and it is I that will meet your needs and refresh your spirit. For just as only one drink of water a day only JUST sustains you, so also when you only come to me once a day do you just barely get sustained. If you want a body that is functioning well, then it takes more than that. It means drinking lots of water throughout the day.

It is the same with me my child. You keep trying to drink your fill once a day instead of drinking from my waters all day long. Each time that you are overwhelmed or when you feel dry - come to me to fill you up again. Sip on my presence all day long instead of waiting for that one moment to fill up again.

As you do this, you will always be topped up. You will always be filled up with my presence. So rest in this now and watch as I fill you up and cause your spirit to overflow so that you can meet the needs of others around you as well.

Do not be afraid, my child, but fill up now and I will cause your way to prosper. Fill up, and you will see that I have not left you dry or barren. Speak to me throughout the day and draw on my strength. Draw on me and you will be filled all of the time. Do this by speaking to me and speaking in tongues. Also do this by listening to me.

As you listen and then pour out, you will have a continual infilling and outpouring. As you do this, you will start to feel fed once again and you will no longer feel dry in your spirit. You will feel at peace and you will no longer struggle to hear my voice. So rest in me today and I will cause your way to prosper. I will cause you to be filled up to overflowing.

Come to me then, my child, and I will show you the way that you must go and the things that you must do. Rest and drink of my presence always in all that you do. Then you will feel peace and joy once again, says the Lord.

Do it Daily

Journal daily for a week, and discuss everything with the Lord from your most intimate fears to thoughts on natural things. The key is to do it often until you get comfortable with it.

Project Submission

1.   Go through all of your journals and pick out one you want to share with your leader. Bring it along to the next meeting.

2.   Remember the first project on Scripture memorization? Brush up on the scriptures you picked out.

3.   Search the Word for additional scriptures relating to any problem or need you have right now and bring those to the next meeting as well. (Doing this makes you accountable and adds some pressure to get yourself into the Word.)

Additional Scriptures:

_____

_____

_____

_____

_____

_____

Outcome Assessment

This project will begin to bring together everything you have learned so far. It combines the Word that you have pushed into your spirit along with the Urim and Thummim and visions. Together, you get a full picture of what the Lord is saying to you right now.

You will begin with types and shadows and then move from there to get clear words of direction. Do not be discouraged if your first try does not come out as you intended – it takes time to "tune in" to the spirit. It takes time to learn to put aside your own ideas and to truly hear what God has to say.

Notes:

_____

_____

_____

_____

_____

_____

_____

_____

_____

_____

Practicing His Presence

Project 8 – Practicing His Presence

Psalms 16:11 You will make known to me the way of life: in your presence [there is] joy that fully satisfies; at your right hand [there are] pleasures that last forever.

Corresponding Chapter

The following project lines up with **Chapter 7: Hearing God Through the Audible and Still Small Voice** from the *How to Hear the Voice of God* book.

It also corresponds with the **Experiencing God's Presence DVD** taken from the *Called to the Ministry* series.

Project Objective

It is our intimacy with Jesus that gives us the strength to face anything that comes our way. As believers though, we tend to work hard at serving the Lord instead of working hard to rest in Him!

It is no surprise that the book of Hebrews tells us to "labor therefore" to enter into His rest! This project is essential for every believer to learn to hear the still small voice within. As you take time to practice His presence, you will be amazed at the clarity you will experience in the spirit and also how much it increases your faith.

You do not realize how often you dwell on things that hinder your faith every day. When you take your eyes off those things and see the Lord in every situation of your life, you will begin to see things differently. Instead of always seeing what cannot be done, you will start having a "possibility thinking." Make this project a new life habit and watch it transform your walk into one of success.

Project Profile

- For leaders in the church
- Essential for the workplace

- When you are under a lot of pressure
- Faith and love builder
- To draw you into an intimate relationship with the Lord
- For those who struggle to express their innermost thoughts and feelings

Project Outline

This project is essentially very simple. Keeping it up however is the challenge – especially when you are under pressure or have a lot coming at you.

What You Do

From the moment you get up in the morning, imagine the Lord Jesus being right there with you. See Him accompanying you to brush your teeth and getting in the car to join you at work.

As you get comfortable with this, converse with the Lord throughout the day. When you wake up, greet Him. When you are on your way to work or doing your chores, tell Him what you are thinking and going through.

Not only will the Lord start becoming very real to you, but you will also start learning to share the inner thoughts of your heart with someone else. Just by unloading these cares, you will feel more equipped to handle the pressures around you.

No matter what you do through the day, until you fall into bed in the evening, imagine the Lord Jesus right there with you. See Him seated across the way from you during dinner and listening intently in your meeting.

The reality is... He is there! He is very interested in your life and wants to be included in it. As you get comfortable with this, you will start to get impressions in your spirit – answers to the questions you are posing to the Lord.

You will start to hear a still small voice responding to your conversation.

It is essential that as you do this project that you keep your conversations with the Lord very casual and real. Do not spend all of your time asking questions or trying to get Him to make decisions for you. No one enjoys a relationship like that!

You are making friends with the Lord here. So here are the three points to keep in mind for this project:

1. Be mindful of the Lord being with you every moment of your day.
2. Converse with the Lord – express your thoughts, opinions, feelings and comments. Give the Lord the "uncensored" version of your thoughts. I promise… He can handle it!
3. Be sensitive to when the Lord responds. Be aware of the still small voice and impressions you get in your spirit as you talk to the Lord.

Project Submission

After practicing the Lord's presence for a week, complete the following questions.

1. How easy or difficult did you find it, sharing the uncensored version of your thoughts with the Lord?

_____

_____

_____

_____

_____

2. What impression did you get of the Lord's personality as you practiced His presence?

_____

_____

_____

_____

3. Share an impression or direction the Lord gave you this week.

_____

_____

_____

_____

4. Share how this project as a whole benefited your spiritual life.

_____

_____

_____

_____

5. Where do you think there is still room for improvement in having this kind of relationship with the Lord?

_____

_____

_____

_____

Outcome Assessment

The best part of this project is that there is never a "completed date." Just like there is always something to look forward to in a natural relationship, so also is there so much you can learn about the Lord.

Never think that you ever get to the place of knowing all of Him. I have known the Lord since I was born in 1974 and I am still discovering aspects of His nature that blow me away. In fact, just when I think that I know Him, He changes things up to remind me that He is an awesome God!

This is what makes this walk so wonderful. There is always more to know about the Lord Jesus. There is always more to experience in Him. There is always more to receive from Him. So take His hand and experience Him from the moment you wake in the morning.

Experience Him as you fall asleep at night. It will change your view of this world. It will change your heart. From there, the sky's the limit!

Notes:

_____

_____

Hearing God Through Circumstances

Project 9 – Hearing God Through Circumstances

Mark 13:29 So you in like manner, when you will see these things come to pass, know that it is near, [even] at the doors.

Corresponding Chapter

The following project lines up with **Chapter 8: Hearing God Through Circumstances** from the *How to Hear the Voice of God* book.

It also corresponds with the **Knowing God's Will DVD** taken from the *Called to the Ministry* series.

Project Objective

After the Lord has spoken in dreams and given you clear direction in your journals, He will back up this revelation through circumstances. Things might start getting uncomfortable! Take the Israelites for example. They cry out to the Lord and so Moses is given the revelation, "You are leaving Egypt!"

Signs followed, and the plagues began. That is not the only thing that happened though. To help the process along, the Lord made sure that Pharaoh made things tough on the Israelites. The message was clear "Egypt is no longer comfortable! It is time to leave!"

Sometimes when the Lord reveals His will through circumstances, it is uncomfortable! However, if you combine that along with the revelation that He has already given to you, you can rest assured that you are in fact hearing His voice.

Now a quick word of caution here: please do not do this project until you have done the others. This project should be considered the capstone that brings them all together. The Lord will not give you circumstances without first speaking to you through journaling, visions or dreams.

He will start nudging you in the direction using the Word and the Spirit first. Once you receive those messages, then He will move on to using circumstance to confirm the direction you should already know.

Many make the mistake on using only circumstances as the voice of God and have made some serious mistakes there. So follow the outline I have given you through this book.

Project Profile

- Fivefold ministers
- Anyone in a leadership position
- A mature believer
- Someone that is familiar with the voice of the Lord
- Ideal family project

Project Outline

Consider something specific that you have been praying about. You are welcome to use anything from the previous projects that you have done in this book.

1. Start With an Outline

Start off by outlining a few things that you have been seeking the Lord about.

_____

_____

_____

_____

_____

2. Revelations so Far

Now as you have worked through these projects, what revelation or impressions has the Lord given you for each of these points?

_____

_____

_____

_____

3. Confirmation Through Others

Has the Lord used others to confirm what you already heard from Him regarding these points? Write down any confirmation you received from others.

_____

_____

_____

_____

4. Confirmation Through Circumstances

Now you are ready to look at your circumstances to see if there are any patterns in your life. Use the table below to clearly document what is going on in your life right now.

As you fill in the table, try to put the points aside that you listed in point 1. The objective here is to take a good look at what is going on around you and to see what is the Lord and what is just the normal course of life.

This project is designed to be done over the course of a week. Now you might not have an answer for every single question for every day of the week. This is alright. The questions are simply designed to jog your memory.

Please use the Table on the next page.

Weekday	Prayer Request
3-5 events that took place at work today	
3-5 events that took place in the home today	
Conflicts you had with people today	
Any old memories that suddenly popped into your mind	

Anything new that happened out of the ordinary	_____ _____ _____ _____ _____ _____ _____
New contacts made with people from the past or someone you did not know	_____ _____ _____ _____ _____ _____ _____
Any sudden change of events today?	_____ _____ _____ _____ _____ _____ _____

Project Submission

Looking at this project as a whole, bring everything together and submit the following report:

1.   Include your list of points of what you have been seeking the Lord about.

_____

_____

_____

_____

_____

_____

2.   Document the revelation the Lord gave you regarding these points.

_____

_____

_____

_____

_____

_____

3.   Include any confirmations received from others.

_____

_____

_____

_____

4.   Now looking through your list of circumstances report the
following:
   a. Which circumstances confirm the revelations that the
         Lord has given to you?

_____

_____

_____

_____

   b. Do you see a pattern in your circumstances through
         this last week? Explain.

_____

_____

_____

_____

    c. What pattern do you see in the conflicts you had with people this week?

_____

_____

_____

_____

    d. What pattern do you see in memories that came to you this week?

_____

_____

_____

_____

5. In conclusion, in one or two sentences, share what you have been seeking the Lord for and what you feel you need to do about it.

_____

_____

_____

_____

Outcome Assessment

This is quite a lengthy project but worth your while. It is also a good time to mention that it might bring up certain patterns that did not relate to what you have been seeking the Lord about.

You will discover more about yourself as you do this project. It will also expose any personal character traits that need to change or inner fears you did not know you had!

That is quite typical of the Holy Spirit – you go in a direction thinking that you "have it covered," only for Him to change that direction completely!

So be open to what the Lord shows you. The confirmation you get through your circumstances might not be what you want it to be! They might go against your flesh. That is why it is important to present this project to someone who can help assess where you are.

It is always good to have someone who has walked with the Lord for a bit to look in from without. So be open to ministry and the input of others.

Notes:

_____

_____

_____

_____

_____

_____

A Final Word
of Blessing

A Final Word of Blessing

I pray that each of these projects has achieved a singular goal – to help you hear the voice of God!

The Lord is speaking to you every day of your life. The Lord Jesus is right by your side, even now, sharing His secrets with you.

All it takes is for you to stop and listen. These pages do not just contain projects – they are habits for life. They are principles that will transform the way you view the Lord and the world around you.

Do not just follow them – make them your own. Allow them to sink into your heart until you are not only hearing God's voice but holding a conversation. That, after all, is the point of this, isn't it? It is not about looking good but about developing a relationship with the one person in this world who loves us more than we love ourselves.

Reach out to Jesus, and He will reach right on back to you. I pray that you enjoy the journey ahead. It has been a privilege to share it with you so far, and I can just imagine the wonderful things that lie ahead of you.

I leave you with a blessing and a deep desire that you are knitted to the Lord as He is knitted to you.

About the Author

Colette Toach

The Master Juggler... Most of the time anyway! Not only is Colette a talented writer with numerous books under her belt, but she is also a full time Mom of four children, awesome cook, powerfully anointed Christian minister/counsel, in your face trainer and an accomplished business woman. Oh yeah, and she still gets to get her beauty sleep every now and again.

Having learnt everything in the trenches and rising through the ranks, Colette brings to the table an all-round understanding to any situation. Having been the follower and then thrust into leadership, she is able to see both sides of the coin and bring a fresh and new understanding. That is why her writings have become such an inspiration and blessing to many who have read her books.

That is why she can boldly challenge anyone, because her motto is "I expect nothing from you I have not done myself!" Her work is not just knowledge but living knowledge.

From humble beginnings in Zimbabwe, Colette spent most of her Childhood and early teen years in South Africa. Having a personal experience and call to the ministry at age 13 and preaching her first sermon at age 14, it is no wonder her path would not be an easy one. Having faced poverty, divorce and rejection, it helped build a strong love for the Lord and compassion for His people. This foundation is what continues to bring forth powerful materials that reach a range of subjects and have helped many to find the unanswered questions they always had without them needing a bachelor's degree to understand it.

As the Co-founder of Apostolic Movement International, LLC, based out of San Diego, California USA, Colette and her husband, along with their team, continue to produce materials, train and hold seminars to help bring change to the Body of Christ, making her a beautiful bride ready for her groom.

How does she do it? She will gladly tell you... By the Lord Jesus' grace alone and in her weakness!

For more about Colette, check out her blog site at: www.colette-toach.com

AMI Recommendations

If you enjoyed this book, we know you will also love the following books on the prophetic.

I'm Not Crazy – I'm a Prophet

By Colette Toach

It takes a prophet to know a prophet!

Only when you have been scorched yourself with this ministry can you appreciate the gold hidden in this book.

You do not have to follow in the footsteps of others before you but can take the wealth of this book and rise above the pit falls.

That is why only Colette can take the prophetic and dish it out in its truth and cover subjects like:

Introduction – Prophets are Crazy!

Chapter 01 – Your Crazy is My Normal

Chapter 02 – Prophets are... Different

Chapter 03 – A Definition of the Prophet

Chapter 04 – The Face-to-Face Relationship with Jesus

Chapter 05 – Welcome to Your Wedding

Chapter 06 – Seven Steps of Entering the Secret Place

Chapter 07 – Aerobics Workout for Prophets

Chapter 08 – Prophetic Landmarks

So are you Crazy?

Maybe a little, but this book will help you to be the true prophet God has called you to be!

How to Get People to Follow You

By Colette Toach

"You have the potential for something magnificent, but until you can get your boat into the water and unfurl those sails... you are not going anywhere. " - Colette Toach

Colette pours out leadership secrets straight from the throneroom that will make you the kind of leader others want to follow. No more hitting your head on the wall. No more being the only one excited about your vision.

Sharing from her own failures and triumphs, Colette hands you the keys to your success as a leader. You will learn:

1. The one thing that will get others to automatically admire you.
2. The two things that keep making people run from your leadership.
3. How to get others excited about your vision.
4. How to get the kind of loyalty that will get others to follow you to the ends of the earth.
5. The 3 phases of God's leadership training - Where are you?
6. How to identify your open doors.
7. How to win the heart of the public.
8. How to win the hearts of those on your team.

Just like Gideon, David, Peter and Moses who weren't born leaders, but were forged into leaders - so you can have the kind of crowd that will follow you anywhere. There is a strong leader inside of you yet. One who is admired, loved and sought out! Learn how to get people to follow you and fulfill the vision that God has given you.

Chapter List:

1. The first Lesson of Leadership
2. The first Three Steps
3. Planning the Journey
4. Time to Set Sail
5. Following the Ark

6. Crossing the Jordan
7. How to get People to Admire You
8. Getting People to Follow 101
9. Keeping those that Follow
10. Winning the Heart of the Public
11. Becoming a Person People Want to Follow
12. Becoming Confident
13. First Stage of Leadership Training: Servanthood
14. Second Stage of Leadership Training: Pressure to Change
15. Third Stage of Leadership Training: Taking on the Load

Fivefold Ministry School

http://www.fivefold-school.com

You Can be a Success in Ministry!

My passion is to see you realize yours! I understand the years in the desert. I know what it feels like to have a fire shut up in your bones, knowing that God has something greater for you.

That is why together, with my husband Craig Toach, we have trained up our own Fivefold Ministry team and in association with apostles all over the world, we hold in our hands the resources to launch you into your ministry!

Not only do we provide specialized fivefold ministry training, we also provide fivefold ministry assessment, personal mentorship, interactive fellowship with other students and once you qualify - certification, credentials and promotion of your ministry.

Here is What We Offer to Prepare You for Your Fivefold Ministry Calling

Identify Your Fivefold Ministry Calling With Free Evaluation

1. If you have not done so already click on the "evaluation" link above and complete the extensive evaluation.
2. Once you are done click the link to have it evaluated by one of our ministers.
3. From there, we will tell you what courses to begin with.

Ministry Certification, Credentials and Ordination

1. To see what program is best suited to you, visit our Degrees page.
2. Temporary credentials are issued to students who have achieved a major in any of our programs.
3. Ordination is offered only by the invitation of the Holy Spirit. As a student qualifies in their course of study, we will seek the Lord on their behalf of their readiness to be released into ministry.
4. Ministry credentials are issued to those who are ordained by the laying on of hands of the A.M.I. leadership.

Ministry Training Materials That Are Totally Unique

1. The materials that you will study were received as a result of revelation received directly from the Lord.
2. All ministry training materials are based squarely on the Scriptures.
3. Every principle taught has been proved by being lived out practically in real fivefold ministry experience by bone-fide fivefold ministers.
4. Since the lessons are based on revelation given to the Church right now along with the experience of fivefold ministers all over the world, you will not find these teachings anywhere else.

Fivefold Ministry Training That Affects More Than Your Mind

1. We put an emphasis on the training aspect of our Fivefold Ministry Training. This is not just head knowledge but wisdom you will live.
2. You will literally live each principle as you learn it.
3. You will become what God called you to be, even if there was no previous evidence of this ministry in you.
4. As a result of additional mentoring, you will move from general ministry on to your full Fivefold Ministry Office in a very short space of time.

Student Only Benefits

1. You will be given a Personal Lecturer who will follow you throughout your training. All our lecturers have been personally mentored by Craig and I and hold at least one fivefold ministry office. A lecturer will be allocated to you according to your calling so that you can be sure that whoever is mentoring you is someone who has gone the way before.
2. Your mentor will be someone who has been along the way and can be there to minister to you, guide you, pray you through and to track your progress. You will be given their contact information so you can keep in touch with them.
3. You will be able to fellowship with other students at the AMI Campus - a place where all students and lecturers network and fellowship.
4. You will be able to get help directly from your lecturers via a special Student Questions Forum
5. Weekly Student Only Chats where our lecturers from around the world train you live - leaving time for questions and hands-on training.

The Way of Dreams & Visions Book with Symbol Dictionary Kit

By Colette Toach

This is the ultimate Dream Kit!

In this kit you are not only getting the teaching you need to understand your dreams and visions, but you are also getting the key to decode them.

Everybody wants to interpret dreams today. However, where is the balance between what the world says and what the Word of God says? You are about to find out that, as a believer, there is a world in the spirit and in the Word that breaks all the boundaries of what you knew - or thought you knew.

This goes beyond dream and vision interpretation; it takes you on a journey into the realm of the spirit.

Did you know that your dreams have a meaning? From the very beginning of time the Lord spoke to His people in dreams and visions. In the New Testament, this ability has become even greater and, instead of a select few, every single believer has the ability to understand what God is saying to them in their dreams.

However, does this mean you have to wait for a dream to hear God? Not at all - Not only can you increase the amount of prophetic dreams you are having, but, you can also learn to receive visions and hear from the Lord at any time.

The Symbol Dictionary included in this kit is one of a kind! Apostle Colette Toach does it again... puts up a standard with an apostolic foundation that you can trust. Refer to this Symbol Dictionary over and over again and find out what God is saying to you in your dreams and visions.

You will refer to this Symbol Dictionary over and over again. You'll never have to look very far for an interpretation again. Simply page through this reference book and get the meaning of the symbols in your dreams and visions.

- Keep it at your bedside and look up what your dream means when you wake up.
- Look up symbols on the go or while you're ministering.

The Lord is talking to you, but do you know what He is saying? Get your copy of the Dreams and Visions Symbol Dictionary today and find out.

Contacting Us

Go to www.ami-bookshop.com to check out our wide selection of materials.

Do you have any questions about any products?

Contact us at: +1 (760) 466 - 7679
(8am to 5pm California Time, Weekdays Only)

E-mail Address: admin@ami-bookshop.com

Postal Address:

A.M.I

5663 Balboa Ave #416

San Diego, CA 92111, USA

AMI Bookshop – It's not Just Knowledge, It's **Living Knowledge**

Made in the USA
San Bernardino, CA
04 October 2014